THE COMPLETE

LOW POTASSIUM COOKBOOK FOR SENIORS

Easy and Delicious Recipes to Manage Hyperkalemia and Improve Your

Kidney Health

Culinary Quill

Copyright

© [Culinary Quill] [2024]

Disclaimer:

The information contained in this book is intended for general informational purposes only and is not a substitute for professional medical advice. Always consult with a healthcare professional regarding any health conditions or before making any changes to your diet or lifestyle.

TABLE OF CONTENTS

Embark on a Culinary Journey

"The Complete Low Potassium Cookbook for Seniors" is your guide to a healthier, happier you. Discover a world of delicious, low-potassium recipes that nourish your body and delight your taste buds. With this cookbook, you'll learn how to manage hyperkalemia, protect your kidneys, and enjoy a vibrant life.

From breakfast to dinner, snacks to desserts, this cookbook offers a variety of options to suit your preferences and dietary needs. With clear instructions, easy-to-follow recipes, and helpful tips, you'll be empowered to take control of your health and create meals that are both delicious and nutritious.

So, what are you waiting for? Turn the page and embark on a culinary journey that will inspire and delight you.

INTRODUCTION

Imagine Patricia, a vibrant senior who once loved to cook but found herself restricted by a recent diagnosis of hyperkalemia. The fear of the unknown, the anxiety of dietary changes, and the overwhelming number of recipes online made her feel lost. She needed a cookbook that not only provided delicious and easy-to-follow recipes but also offered a clear path to managing her condition.

A common health concern among seniors, hyperkalemia occurs when there's an excessive amount of potassium in the blood. This can lead to serious health complications, including heart problems.

"The Complete Low Potassium Cookbook for Seniors" is your guide to navigating hyperkalemia and enjoying delicious, flavorful meals. With carefully curated recipes designed to be both low in potassium and packed with taste, this cookbook empowers you to take control of your health and maintain a vibrant lifestyle.

As a renowned expert in the field of nutrition and senior health, [Culinary Quill] brings years of experience and passion to this cookbook. With a deep understanding of the challenges faced by seniors with hyperkalemia, [Culinary Quill] has created a collection of recipes that are not only delicious but also easy to prepare and follow.

The Benefits:

Improved kidney health: A low-potassium diet can help protect your kidneys and prevent further complications.

Enhanced well-being: By managing hyperkalemia, you can experience increased energy, better sleep, and overall improved quality of life.

Delicious and satisfying meals: Our recipes are designed to be flavorful and enjoyable, so you can savor every bite without compromising your health.

Easy-to-follow instructions: Our recipes are written with seniors in mind, providing clear and concise instructions that are easy to understand and follow.

Taking control of your health is essential. With "The Complete Low Potassium Cookbook for Seniors," you have the tools and knowledge to enjoy a fulfilling life while managing hyperkalemia.

Start your journey to better health today! Order your copy of **"The Complete Low Potassium Cookbook for Seniors"** and discover a world of delicious, low-potassium recipes tailored to your needs.

PART 1: THE BASICS

Essential Ingredients and Equipment

- **Low-potassium fruits and vegetables:** Apples, blueberries, grapes, peaches, pears, carrots, cucumbers, green beans, bell peppers, spinach, zucchini, and mushrooms are all good options.

- **Lean proteins:** Chicken, fish, turkey, eggs, tofu, and tempeh are excellent sources of protein that are low in potassium.

- **Whole grains:** Brown rice, quinoa, and whole-grain bread are healthy and filling options.

- **Dairy alternatives:** Low-fat or fat-free milk, yogurt, and cheese made from almonds, soy, or coconut can be used as substitutes for traditional dairy products.

- **Low-potassium seasonings:** Herbs, spices, garlic powder, onion powder, and lemon juice can add flavor to your dishes without adding excess potassium.

- **Low-potassium sweeteners:** Stevia, monk fruit extract, and erythritol are natural sweeteners that are low in potassium.

Essential Equipment for Low-Potassium Cooking

- **Measuring cups and spoons:** To accurately measure ingredients and control potassium intake.

- **Cutting board and knife:** For preparing fruits, vegetables, and proteins.

- **Saucepans and skillets:** For cooking a variety of dishes.

- **Baking sheets and pans:** For roasting vegetables and baking dishes.

- **Blender or food processor:** For making smoothies, sauces, and purees.

- **Kitchen timer:** To ensure food is cooked to the appropriate temperature.

- **Food scale:** To accurately measure ingredients, especially for those with dietary restrictions.

By stocking your kitchen with these essential ingredients and equipment, you can easily prepare delicious and nutritious low-potassium meals that are perfect for seniors.

Understanding Potassium Levels in Foods

Potassium is a vital mineral for the body, but it can be harmful in excess for individuals with certain health conditions, such as kidney disease. To maintain a low-potassium diet, it's essential to understand which foods are high in this mineral.

Here are some general guidelines to help you identify high-potassium foods:

Fruits:

- **High potassium:** Bananas, cantaloupe, dried fruits (apricots, raisins, prunes), grapefruit, honeydew melon, nectarines, oranges, papayas, and prunes.

- **Moderate potassium:** Apples, berries (blueberries, strawberries, raspberries), cherries, grapes, peaches, pears, and plums.

Vegetables:

- **High potassium:** Potatoes, sweet potatoes, spinach, kale, beet greens, collard greens, Swiss chard, avocado, and tomatoes.
- **Moderate potassium:** Carrots, cucumbers, green beans, broccoli, cauliflower, bell peppers, onions, and zucchini.

Dairy Products:

- **High potassium:** Milk, yogurt, and cheese.
- **Low potassium:** Low-fat or fat-free dairy alternatives (soy, almond, coconut)

Legumes and Beans:

- **High potassium:** White beans, kidney beans, lima beans, chickpeas, and lentils.

Nuts and Seeds:

- **High potassium:** Almonds, cashews, pistachios, sunflower seeds, and pumpkin seeds.
- Processed Foods:
- **High potassium:** Many processed foods, such as canned soups, canned vegetables, and processed meats, can be high in potassium.

Tips for Identifying High-Potassium Foods:

- **Read food labels:** Check the nutrition facts label for potassium content.

- **Use a food database:** Online resources can provide detailed information about the potassium content of different foods.

- **Be aware of hidden sources:** Potassium can be added to processed foods as a preservative.

- **Consult a healthcare professional:** If you have specific dietary needs or health concerns, consult a registered dietitian or healthcare provider for personalized guidance.

By understanding these guidelines and making informed choices, you can effectively manage your potassium intake and maintain a healthy diet.

Additional Thoughts:

- **Find joy in the kitchen:** Cooking can be a therapeutic and enjoyable activity. Experiment with different flavors, techniques, and ingredients to discover new favorites.

- **Involve loved ones:** Cooking can be a social activity. Invite friends or family members to join you in the kitchen and create delicious meals together.

- **Be patient with yourself:** Making dietary changes takes time. Don't be discouraged if you encounter setbacks. Focus on progress, not perfection.

- **Honor your accomplishments:** Recognize your accomplishments, no matter how minor. Every action you take in the direction of a healthy way of living is a triumph.

PART 2: BREAKFAST RECIPES

Oatmeal with Berries and Nuts

Short Description: A hearty and healthy breakfast option that is low in potassium and packed with nutrients.

Ingredients:

- 1/2 cup rolled oats

- 1 cup low-potassium milk (almond, oat, or soy)

- 1/4 teaspoon ground cinnamon

- 1/4 teaspoon ground nutmeg

- 1/4 cup mixed berries (blueberries, strawberries, raspberries)

- 1 tablespoon chopped nuts (almonds, walnuts, pecans)

- Sweetener to taste (stevia, monk fruit extract, or honey)

Instructions:

1. In a small saucepan, combine oats, milk, cinnamon, and nutmeg.

2. Bring to a boil, then reduce heat and simmer for 3-5 minutes, or until oats are tender.

3. Stir in berries and nuts.

4. Sweeten to taste.

Cook Time: 5-7 minutes | **Prep Time:** 5 minutes | **Portion Size:** 1 serving

Nutritional Facts per Meal (approximate):

Calories: 250-300

Protein: 7-10 grams

Carbohydrates: 35-40 grams

Fiber: 5-7 grams

Potassium: Low

Diet Ideas:

1. For a vegan option, use plant-based milk and omit honey.

2. For a gluten-free option, use gluten-free oats.

3. For added protein, top with a scoop of protein powder.

4. For a nut-free option, omit nuts and add a tablespoon of chia seeds.

Scrambled Eggs with Spinach and Avocado

Short Description: A quick and easy breakfast option that is low in potassium and packed with protein.

Ingredients:

- 2 large eggs

- 1/4 cup chopped spinach

- 1/4 avocado, diced

- Salt and pepper to taste

- 1 tablespoon butter or olive oil

Instructions:

1. In a small skillet, melt butter or olive oil over medium heat.

2. Add spinach and cook until wilted.

3. Add eggs and scramble until cooked to your desired consistency.

4. Stir in avocado and season with salt and pepper.

Cook Time: 5-7 minutes | **Prep Time:** 5 minutes | **Portion Size:** 1 serving

Nutritional Facts per Meal (approximate):

Calories: 200-250

Protein: 15-20 grams

Carbohydrates: 5-10 grams

Fat: 15-20 grams

Potassium: Low

Diet Ideas:

1. For a vegetarian option, use a plant-based egg substitute.

2. For a low-fat option, use less butter or olive oil.

3. For added flavor, add a sprinkle of feta cheese.

4. For a whole-grain option, serve with a slice of whole-grain toast.

Rice Pudding with Cinnamon

Short Description: A creamy and comforting breakfast option that is low in potassium and easy to digest.

Ingredients:
- 1/2 cup rice (arborio or jasmine)
- 1 cup low-potassium milk (almond, oat, or soy)
- 1/4 teaspoon ground cinnamon
- 1/4 teaspoon ground nutmeg
- Sweetener to taste (stevia, monk fruit extract, or honey)
- Optional toppings: berries, nuts, or a drizzle of maple syrup

Instructions:
1. In a small saucepan, combine rice, milk, cinnamon, and nutmeg.

2. Bring to a boil, then reduce heat and simmer for 20-25 minutes, or until rice is tender

and the mixture thickens.

3. Stir in sweetener to taste.

4. Serve warm, topped with your desired toppings.

Cook Time: 20-25 minutes | **Prep Time:** 5 minutes | **Portion Size:** 1 serving

Nutritional Facts per Meal (approximate):

Calories: 200-250

Protein: 5-7 grams

Carbohydrates: 30-35 grams

Fiber: 2-3 grams

Potassium: Low

Diet Ideas:

1. For a vegan option, use plant-based milk and omit honey.

2. For a gluten-free option, use gluten-free rice.

3. For added protein, top with a scoop of protein powder.

4. For a nut-free option, omit nuts.

Green and Creamy Smoothie

Short Description: A refreshing and nutritious smoothie that is low in potassium and packed with vitamins and minerals.

Ingredients:

- 1 cup spinach
- 1 banana, peeled and sliced
- 1 cup almond milk
- 1 tablespoon chia seeds (optional)
- 1 teaspoon honey (optional)

Instructions:

1. Combine all ingredients in a blender.
2. Blend until smooth.
3. Pour into a glass and enjoy immediately.

Cook Time: 5 minutes | **Prep Time:** 5 minutes | **Portion Size:** 1 serving

Nutritional Facts per Meal (approximate):

Calories: 200-250

Protein: 7-10 grams

Carbohydrates: 30-35 grams

Fiber: 5-7 grams

Potassium: Low

Diet Ideas:

1. For a vegan option, use plant-based almond milk and honey.

2. For a nut-free option, use a different type of milk, such as oat or soy.

3. For added protein, add a scoop of protein powder.

4. For a thicker smoothie, add more chia seeds.

Avocado Toast with a Fried Egg

Short Description: A classic and satisfying breakfast option that is low in potassium and packed with protein and healthy fats.

Ingredients:

- 1 slice whole-grain bread

- 1/2 avocado, mashed

- 1 egg

- Salt and pepper to taste

- 1 tablespoon butter or olive oil

Instructions:

1. Toast the bread to your desired level.

2. Spread the mashed avocado on the toasted bread.

3. In a small skillet, melt butter or olive oil over medium heat.

4. Crack the egg into the skillet and cook until the whites are set and the yolk is cooked to your desired level.

5. Place the fried egg on top of the avocado toast and season with salt and pepper.

Cook Time: 5-7 minutes | **Prep Time:** 5 minutes | **Portion Size:** 1 serving

Nutritional Facts per Meal (approximate):

Calories: 250-300

Protein: 15-20 grams

Carbohydrates: 25-30 grams

Fat: 15-20 grams

Potassium: Low

Diet Ideas:

1. For a vegan option, use a plant-based egg substitute.

2. For a low-fat option, use less butter or olive oil.

3. For added flavor, sprinkle with red pepper flakes or a squeeze of lemon juice.

4. For a whole-grain option, use a thicker slice of whole-grain bread.

Cottage Cheese Parfait

Short Description: A simple and nutritious breakfast option that is low in potassium and packed with protein.

Ingredients:

- 1/2 cup cottage cheese
- 1/2 cup mixed berries (blueberries, strawberries, raspberries)
- 1 tablespoon chopped nuts (almonds, walnuts, pecans)
- Sweetener to taste (stevia, monk fruit extract, or honey)

Instructions:

1. In a small bowl, combine cottage cheese, berries, and nuts.
2. Stir in sweetener to taste.

Prep Time: 5 minutes | **Portion Size:** 1 serving

Nutritional Facts per Meal (approximate):

Calories: 150-200

Protein: 15-20 grams

Carbohydrates: 20-25 grams

Fat: 5-10 grams

Potassium: Low

Diet Ideas:

1. For a vegan option, use plant-based cottage cheese.

2. For a nut-free option, omit nuts.

3. For added protein, top with a scoop of protein powder.

4. For a thicker parfait, add a spoonful of Greek yogurt.

Almond Flour Pancakes

Short Description: A delicious and fluffy breakfast option that is low in potassium and gluten-free.

Ingredients:

- 1/2 cup almond flour

- 2 large eggs

- 1/4 cup milk (almond, oat, or soy)

- 1 teaspoon baking powder

- 1/4 teaspoon baking soda

- 1/4 teaspoon salt

- Sweetener to taste (stevia, monk fruit extract, or honey)

Instructions:

1. In a small bowl, whisk together almond flour, eggs, milk, baking powder, baking soda, and salt.

2. Stir in sweetener to taste.

3. Heat a non-stick skillet over medium heat.

4. Pour 1/4 cup of batter onto the skillet and cook for 2-3 minutes per side, or until golden brown.

5. Serve with your favorite toppings, such as berries, maple syrup, or a sprinkle of cinnamon.

Cook Time: 10-15 minutes | **Prep Time:** 5 minutes | **Portion Size:** 2-3 pancakes

Nutritional Facts per Meal (approximate):

Calories: 200-250

Protein: 10-15 grams

Carbohydrates: 20-25 grams

Fat: 10-15 grams

Potassium: Low

Diet Ideas:

1. For a vegan option, use plant-based eggs and milk.

2. For a nut-free option, use a different type of flour, such as coconut flour.

3. For added protein, top with a scoop of protein powder.

4. For a thicker pancake, add more almond flour.

Fruit and Yogurt Parfait

Short Description: A refreshing and nutritious breakfast option that is low in potassium and packed with protein.

Ingredients:

- 1/2 cup Greek yogurt
- 1/2 cup mixed berries (blueberries, strawberries, raspberries)
- 1/4 cup granola (low-potassium option)
- Honey or maple syrup to taste

Instructions:

1. In a glass or bowl, layer the yogurt, berries, and granola.

2. Drizzle with honey or maple syrup to taste.

Prep Time: 5 minutes | **Portion Size:** 1 serving

Nutritional Facts per Meal (approximate):

Calories: 200-250

Protein: 15-20 grams

Carbohydrates: 30-35 grams

Fat: 5-10 grams

Potassium: Low

Diet Ideas:

1. For a vegan option, use plant-based yogurt and granola.

2. For a nut-free option, choose a granola without nuts.

3. For added protein, top with a scoop of protein powder.

4. For a thicker parfait, add a spoonful of chia seeds.

Classic Hard-Boiled Eggs with Whole-Grain Toast

Short Description: A simple and satisfying breakfast option that is low in potassium and packed with protein.

Ingredients:

- 2 large eggs

- 1 slice whole-grain bread

- Salt and pepper to taste

Instructions:

1. Place eggs in a saucepan and cover with cold water.

2. Bring to a boil, then reduce heat and simmer for 10-12 minutes.

3. Drain the water and run cold water over the eggs to cool them down.

4. Peel the eggs and serve with whole-grain toast, seasoned with salt and pepper.

Cook Time: 15-20 minutes | **Prep Time:** 5 minutes | **Portion Size:** 1 serving

Nutritional Facts per Meal (approximate):

Calories: 200-250

Protein: 15-20 grams

Carbohydrates: 25-30 grams

Fat: 10-15 grams

Potassium: Low

Diet Ideas:

1. For added flavor, top the eggs with a sprinkle of paprika or a drizzle of hot sauce.

2. For a vegetarian option, use a plant-based egg substitute.

3. For a whole-grain option, use a thicker slice of whole-grain bread.

4. For a low-fat option, use a light version of whole-grain bread.

Whole-Grain Waffles with Fruit and Syrup

Short Description: A delicious and indulgent breakfast option that is low in potassium and packed with flavor.

Ingredients:

- 1 cup whole-grain waffle mix
- 1 cup low-potassium milk (almond, oat, or soy)
- 1 egg
- 1 tablespoon melted butter
- 1/2 teaspoon vanilla extract
- 1/2 cup mixed berries (blueberries, strawberries, raspberries)
- Maple syrup or honey to taste

Instructions:

1. In a bowl, whisk together waffle mix, milk, egg, butter, and vanilla extract.
2. Pour batter into a waffle iron and cook according to manufacturer's instructions.
3. Serve waffles with berries and maple syrup or honey.

Cook Time: 10-15 minutes | **Prep Time:** 5 minutes | **Portion Size:** 1 waffle

Nutritional Facts per Meal (approximate):

Calories: 250-300

Protein: 10-15 grams

Carbohydrates: 30-35 grams

Fat: 10-15 grams

Potassium: Low

Diet Ideas:

1. For a vegan option, use plant-based milk and eggs.

2. For a nut-free option, ensure the waffle mix does not contain nuts.

3. For added protein, top with a scoop of protein powder.

4. For a thicker waffle, add more batter.

Additional Breakfast Tips

- **Make it a priority:** Start your day with a nourishing breakfast to fuel your body and mind.

- **Customize your recipes:** Experiment with different ingredients and flavors to find your favorite combinations.

- **Prepare ahead:** If you're short on time, prepare your breakfast the night before.

- **Consider your individual needs:** If you have specific dietary needs or preferences, adjust the recipes accordingly.

- **Enjoy the process:** Breakfast should be a pleasurable experience. Take your time and savor each bite.

PART 3: LUNCH RECIPES

Grilled Chicken Salad

Short Description: A light and refreshing lunch option that is low in potassium and packed with protein.

Ingredients:

- 1 boneless, skinless chicken breast
- 1 cup mixed greens
- 1/2 cup chopped cucumber
- 1/4 cup chopped tomato
- 1/4 cup chopped red onion
- Low-potassium salad dressing of your choice
- Salt and pepper to taste

Instructions:

1. Season chicken breast with salt and pepper.
2. Grill or broil chicken until cooked through. Let cool, then slice into strips.
3. In a large bowl, combine greens, cucumber, tomato, and red onion.
4. Add grilled chicken strips and toss to coat with salad dressing.

Cook Time: 20-25 minutes | **Prep Time:** 15 minutes | **Portion Size:** 1 serving

Nutritional Facts per Meal (approximate):

Calories: 300-350

Protein: 30-35 grams

Carbohydrates: 20-25 grams

Fat: 15-20 grams

Potassium: Low

Diet Ideas:

1. For a vegetarian option, substitute grilled chicken with grilled tofu or tempeh.

2. For a low-fat option, use a light or vinaigrette-based salad dressing.

3. For added flavor, sprinkle with feta cheese or a squeeze of lemon juice.

4. For a whole-grain option, serve with a side of whole-grain crackers or bread.

Chicken Taco Bowls

Short Description: A flavorful and satisfying lunch option that is low in potassium and packed with protein.

Ingredients:

- 1 boneless, skinless chicken breast

- 1 tablespoon taco seasoning

- 1 cup cooked brown rice

- 1/2 cup black beans, rinsed and drained

- 1/4 cup diced red onion

- 1/4 cup diced green bell pepper

- 1/4 cup chopped cilantro

- Low-potassium salsa

- Avocado, diced (optional)

- Tortilla chips (optional)

Instructions:

1. Season chicken breast with taco seasoning.

2. Grill or broil chicken until cooked through. Let cool, then shred.

3. In a bowl, combine brown rice, black beans, red onion, green bell pepper, and cilantro.

4. Top with shredded chicken, salsa, and diced avocado (if desired).

5. Serve with tortilla chips, if desired.

Cook Time: 20-25 minutes | **Prep Time:** 15 minutes | **Portion Size:** 1 serving

Nutritional Facts per Meal (approximate):

Calories: 400-450

Protein: 30-35 grams

Carbohydrates: 40-45 grams

Fat: 15-20 grams

Potassium: Low

Diet Ideas:

1. For a vegetarian option, substitute chicken with grilled tofu or tempeh.

2. For a gluten-free option, use gluten-free tortilla chips.

3. For a low-fat option, use a light or salsa-based dressing.

4. For added flavor, sprinkle with feta cheese or a squeeze of lime juice.

Corn Fritters

Short Description: A crispy and flavorful lunch option that is low in potassium and packed with whole grains.

Ingredients:

- 1 cup canned corn, drained

- 1/2 cup all-purpose flour

- 1 egg

- 1/4 teaspoon baking powder

- 1/4 teaspoon salt

- 1 tablespoon melted butter

- 1/4 cup chopped cilantro

- Optional toppings: salsa, sour cream, or avocado

Instructions:

1. In a bowl, combine corn, flour, egg, baking powder, salt, and butter. Stir until well combined.

2. Stir in cilantro.

3. Heat a skillet over medium heat. Drop 1/4 cup of batter into the skillet for each fritter.

4. Cook for 2-3 minutes per side, or until golden brown.

5. Serve hot with your desired toppings.

Cook Time: 15-20 minutes | **Prep Time:** 10 minutes | **Portion Size:** 3-4 fritters

Nutritional Facts per Meal (approximate):

Calories: 200-250

Protein: 5-7 grams

Carbohydrates: 30-35 grams

Fat: 10-15 grams

Potassium: Low

Diet Ideas:

1. For a gluten-free option, use gluten-free flour.

2. For a vegan option, use plant-based egg substitute.

3. For added flavor, add a pinch of chili powder or cumin.

4. For a healthier option, serve with a side of grilled vegetables.

Tuna Salad Sandwich on Whole-Grain Bread

Short Description: A classic and satisfying lunch option that is low in potassium and packed with protein.

Ingredients:

- 1 (5-ounce) can tuna in water, drained
- 1/4 cup mayonnaise
- 1/4 cup chopped celery
- 1/4 cup chopped onion
- 1 tablespoon lemon juice
- Salt and pepper to taste
- 2 slices whole-grain bread

Instructions:

1. In a bowl, combine tuna, mayonnaise, celery, onion, lemon juice, salt, and pepper. Mix well.

2. Spread tuna salad on both sides of whole-grain bread.

3. Serve immediately.

Prep Time: 10 minutes | **Portion Size:** 1 sandwich

Nutritional Facts per Meal (approximate):

Calories: 300-350

Protein: 20-25 grams

Carbohydrates: 30-35 grams

Fat: 15-20 grams

Potassium: Low

Diet Ideas:

1. For a vegetarian option, use a plant-based tuna alternative.

2. For a low-fat option, use light mayonnaise or Greek yogurt instead of mayonnaise.

3. For added flavor, add chopped dill or parsley.

4. For a whole-grain option, use a thicker slice of whole-grain bread.

Vegetable Frittata

Short Description: A hearty and flavorful lunch option that is low in potassium and packed with protein.

Ingredients:

- 6 large eggs, beaten
- 1 cup chopped spinach
- 1/2 cup chopped red onion
- 1/4 cup chopped bell pepper
- 1/4 cup grated Parmesan cheese
- Salt and pepper to taste
- 1 tablespoon olive oil

Instructions:

1. Preheat oven to 350°F (175°C).
2. In a large bowl, combine eggs, spinach, onion, bell pepper, Parmesan cheese, salt, and pepper.
3. Heat olive oil in a 9-inch oven-safe skillet over medium heat.
4. Pour egg mixture into skillet and cook for 2-3 minutes, or until set on the bottom.
5. Place skillet in preheated oven and bake for 10-15 minutes, or until the frittata is set and golden brown.

6. Let cool slightly before cutting into slices.

Cook Time: 20-25 minutes | **Prep Time:** 15 minutes | **Portion Size:** 4 servings

Nutritional Facts per Meal (approximate):

Calories: 250-300

Protein: 20-25 grams

Carbohydrates: 10-15 grams

Fat: 15-20 grams

Potassium: Low

Diet Ideas:

1. For a vegetarian option, use a plant-based egg substitute.

2. For a low-fat option, use less olive oil or a non-stick skillet.

3. For added flavor, sprinkle with fresh herbs like basil or oregano.

4. For a whole-grain option, serve with a side of whole-grain toast.

Leftovers from Dinner

Short Description: A quick and easy lunch option that is low in potassium and helps to reduce food waste.

Ingredients:

- Leftover dinner dish of your choice (e.g., roasted chicken, grilled salmon, vegetable stir-fry)

- Whole-grain bread or wrap

- Optional toppings: lettuce, tomato, cheese, avocado

Instructions:

1. Place leftover dinner dish on a plate.

2. Serve with whole-grain bread or wrap.

3. Add your desired toppings.

Prep Time: 5-10 minutes | **Portion Size:** 1 serving

Nutritional Facts per Meal (approximate):

Varies depending on the leftover dish.

Generally low in potassium.

Diet Ideas:

1. Choose a leftover dish that is low in potassium and high in protein.

2. Add vegetables to your leftover dish for extra nutrients.

3. Serve with a side salad or fruit for added fiber and vitamins.

Vegetable Wrap with Hummus

Short Description: A healthy and satisfying lunch option that is low in potassium and packed with nutrients.

Ingredients:

- 1 whole-grain wrap
- 1/4 cup hummus
- 1/2 cup chopped spinach
- 1/4 cup chopped cucumber
- 1/4 cup chopped red onion
- Optional toppings: shredded carrots, avocado, feta cheese

Instructions:

1. Spread hummus on the whole-grain wrap.
2. Add spinach, cucumber, and red onion.
3. Roll up the wrap and enjoy.

Prep Time: 5-10 minutes | **Portion Size:** 1 wrap

Nutritional Facts per Meal (approximate):

Calories: 250-300

Protein: 10-15 grams

Carbohydrates: 30-35 grams

Fat: 10-15 grams

Potassium: Low

Diet Ideas:

1. For a vegan option, use plant-based hummus.

2. For a low-fat option, use a light or reduced-fat hummus.

3. For added flavor, sprinkle with paprika or a squeeze of lemon juice.

4. For a whole-grain option, use a thicker whole-grain wrap.

Grilled Cheese with Avocado

Short Description: A classic and satisfying lunch option that is low in potassium and packed with protein and healthy fats.

Ingredients:

- 2 slices whole-grain bread

- 1/4 cup shredded cheese (cheddar, mozzarella, or provolone)

- 1/4 avocado, mashed

- 1 tablespoon butter or olive oil

Instructions:

1. Spread mashed avocado on one side of a slice of whole-grain bread.

2. Top with shredded cheese.

3. Place the other slice of bread on top and butter both sides.

4. Grill or pan-fry the sandwich until golden brown and the cheese is melted.

Cook Time: 5-7 minutes | **Prep Time:** 5 minutes | **Portion Size:** 1 sandwich

Nutritional Facts per Meal (approximate):

Calories: 250-300

Protein: 15-20 grams

Carbohydrates: 25-30 grams

Fat: 15-20 grams

Potassium: Low

Diet Ideas:

1. For a vegan option, use plant-based cheese.

2. For a low-fat option, use less butter or olive oil.

3. For added flavor, sprinkle with red pepper flakes or a squeeze of lemon juice.

4. For a whole-grain option, use a thicker slice of whole-grain bread.

Additional Lunch Tips

- **Pack a lunch:** Preparing your lunch ahead of time can save you money and help you make healthier choices.

- **Don't be afraid to experiment:** Try new recipes and ingredients to keep your meals interesting and enjoyable.

- **Listen to your body:** Pay attention to your hunger cues and eat when you're truly hungry.

- **Mindful eating:** Take your time and savor each bite. Enjoy the flavors and textures of your food.

- **Stay hydrated:** Drink plenty of water throughout the day to stay hydrated and support digestion.

- **Share a meal with a friend:** Eating with others can make mealtime more enjoyable and social.

- **Don't be afraid to ask for help:** If you're struggling to create low-potassium lunch options, don't hesitate to reach out to a registered dietitian or healthcare provider for guidance.

PART 4: DINNER RECIPES

Baked Chicken with Roasted Vegetables

Short Description: A flavorful and healthy dinner option that is low in potassium and packed with protein and nutrients.

Ingredients:

- 1 boneless, skinless chicken breast

- 1 tablespoon olive oil

- 1/2 cup chopped broccoli florets

- 1/2 cup chopped carrots

- 1/4 cup chopped red onion

- 1/4 teaspoon dried thyme

- 1/4 teaspoon dried rosemary

- Salt and pepper to taste

Instructions:

1. Preheat oven to 400°F (200°C).

2. Season chicken breast with salt and pepper.

3. Drizzle olive oil over chicken and vegetables.

4. Toss to coat and arrange on a baking sheet.

5. Sprinkle with thyme and rosemary.

6. Bake for 20-25 minutes, or until chicken is cooked through and vegetables are tender.

Cook Time: 20-25 minutes | **Prep Time:** 15 minutes | **Portion Size:** 1 serving

Nutritional Facts per Meal (approximate):

Calories: 300-350

Protein: 30-35 grams

Carbohydrates: 20-25 grams

Fat: 15-20 grams

Potassium: Low

Diet Ideas:

1. For a vegetarian option, substitute chicken with tofu or tempeh.

2. For a low-fat option, use less olive oil.

3. For added flavor, sprinkle with Parmesan cheese or a squeeze of lemon juice.

4. For a whole-grain option, serve with a side of brown rice or quinoa.

Salmon with Roasted Asparagus and Quinoa

Short Description: A healthy and flavorful dinner option that is low in potassium and packed with protein and nutrients.

Ingredients:

- 1 salmon fillet
- 1 bunch asparagus, trimmed
- 1 cup cooked quinoa
- 1 tablespoon olive oil
- 1/4 teaspoon dried dill
- 1/4 teaspoon dried parsley
- Salt and pepper to taste

Instructions:

1. Preheat oven to 400°F (200°C).
2. Season salmon with salt and pepper.
3. Drizzle olive oil over asparagus.
4. Toss to coat and arrange on a baking sheet with salmon.
5. Sprinkle with dill and parsley.
6. Bake for 15-20 minutes, or until salmon is cooked through and asparagus is tender.
7. Serve salmon and asparagus with cooked quinoa.

Cook Time: 15-20 minutes | **Prep Time:** 10 minutes | **Portion Size:** 1 serving

Nutritional Facts per Meal (approximate):

Calories: 350-400

Protein: 30-35 grams

Carbohydrates: 30-35 grams

Fat: 20-25 grams

Potassium: Low

Diet Ideas:

1. For a vegetarian option, substitute salmon with tofu or tempeh.

2. For a low-fat option, use less olive oil.

3. For added flavor, sprinkle with lemon zest or a squeeze of lemon juice.

4. For a whole-grain option, use a different type of grain instead of quinoa.

Beef Stir-Fry with Brown Rice

Short Description: A flavorful and satisfying dinner option that is low in potassium and packed with protein.

Ingredients:

- 1 pound boneless, skinless beef stir-fry strips

- 1 tablespoon olive oil

- 1/2 cup chopped broccoli florets

- 1/2 cup chopped carrots

- 1/4 cup chopped red onion

- 1/4 cup soy sauce (low-sodium)

- 1 tablespoon rice vinegar

- 1 teaspoon cornstarch

- 1 cup cooked brown rice

- Salt and pepper to taste

Instructions:

1. Season beef with salt and pepper.

2. Heat olive oil in a large skillet over medium-high heat.

3. Add beef and cook until browned. Remove from skillet and set aside.

4. Add vegetables to skillet and cook until tender-crisp.

5. Return beef to skillet and add soy sauce, rice vinegar, and cornstarch. Stir to coat.

6. Cook for 1-2 minutes, or until sauce thickens.

7. Serve over cooked brown rice.

Cook Time: 20-25 minutes | **Prep Time:** 15 minutes | **Portion Size:** 1 serving

Nutritional Facts per Meal (approximate):

Calories: 400-450

Protein: 30-35 grams

Carbohydrates: 35-40 grams

Fat: 15-20 grams

Potassium: Low

Diet Ideas:

1. For a vegetarian option, substitute beef with tofu or tempeh.

2. For a low-sodium option, use a reduced-sodium soy sauce.

3. For added flavor, sprinkle with sesame seeds or chopped scallions.

4. For a whole-grain option, use a different type of brown rice.

Lentil Soup with Whole-Grain Bread

Short Description: A hearty and comforting dinner option that is low in potassium and packed with protein and fiber.

Ingredients:

- 1 cup dried lentils, rinsed and sorted

- 4 cups vegetable broth

- 1 onion, chopped

- 1 carrot, chopped

- 1 celery stalk, chopped

- 1 clove garlic, minced

- 1 bay leaf

- Salt and pepper to taste

- Whole-grain bread

Instructions:

1. In a large pot, combine lentils, vegetable broth, onion, carrot, celery, garlic, and bay leaf.

2. Bring to a boil, then reduce heat and simmer for 20-25 minutes, or until lentils are tender.

3. Remove from heat and discard bay leaf.

4. Season with salt and pepper to taste.

5. Serve hot with whole-grain bread.

Cook Time: 30-35 minutes | **Prep Time:** 15 minutes | **Portion Size:** 1 serving

Nutritional Facts per Meal (approximate):

Calories: 300-350

Protein: 20-25 grams

Carbohydrates: 40-45 grams

Fat: 5-10 grams

Potassium: Low

Diet Ideas:

1. For a vegetarian option, use vegetable broth and lentils.

2. For a low-sodium option, use reduced-sodium vegetable broth.

3. For added flavor, add a pinch of chili powder or cumin.

4. For a whole-grain option, use a thicker slice of whole-grain bread.

Leftover Pasta with Tomato Sauce and Vegetables

Short Description: A quick and easy dinner option that is low in potassium and helps to reduce food waste.

Ingredients:

*   Leftover pasta (whole-grain or gluten-free)

*   Leftover tomato sauce

*   Leftover vegetables (e.g., broccoli, carrots, spinach)

*   Parmesan cheese (optional)

Instructions:

1. Heat leftover tomato sauce in a saucepan.

2. Add leftover pasta and vegetables.

3. Toss to coat and heat through.

4. Serve with Parmesan cheese, if desired.

Cook Time: 5-10 minutes | **Prep Time:** 5 minutes | **Portion Size:** 1 serving

Nutritional Facts per Meal (approximate):

Varies depending on the leftover ingredients.

Generally low in potassium.

Diet Ideas:

1. Choose a leftover pasta that is whole-grain or gluten-free.

2. Add more vegetables to your leftover dish for extra nutrients.

3. Serve with a side salad or fruit for added fiber and vitamins.

Grilled Chicken with Roasted Vegetables

Short Description: A flavorful and healthy dinner option that is low in potassium and packed with protein and nutrients.

Ingredients:

- 1 boneless, skinless chicken breast
- 1 tablespoon olive oil
- 1/2 cup chopped broccoli florets
- 1/2 cup chopped carrots
- 1/4 cup chopped red onion
- 1/4 teaspoon dried thyme
- 1/4 teaspoon dried rosemary
- Salt and pepper to taste

Instructions:

1. Preheat oven to 400°F (200°C).
2. Season chicken breast with salt and pepper.
3. Drizzle olive oil over chicken and vegetables.
4. Toss to coat and arrange on a baking sheet.
5. Sprinkle with thyme and rosemary.
6. Bake for 20-25 minutes, or until chicken is cooked through and vegetables are tender.

Cook Time: 20-25 minutes | **Prep Time:** 15 minutes | **Portion Size:** 1 serving

Nutritional Facts per Meal (approximate):

Calories: 300-350

Protein: 30-35 grams

Carbohydrates: 20-25 grams

Fat: 15-20 grams

Potassium: Low

Diet Ideas:

1. For a vegetarian option, substitute chicken with tofu or tempeh.

2. For a low-fat option, use less olive oil.

3. For added flavor, sprinkle with Parmesan cheese or a squeeze of lemon juice.

4. For a whole-grain option, serve with a side of brown rice or quinoa.

Quinoa Bowl with Roasted Vegetables and Tofu

Short Description: A hearty and satisfying dinner option that is low in potassium and packed with protein and nutrients.

Ingredients:

- 1 cup cooked quinoa

- 1/2 cup chopped broccoli florets

- 1/2 cup chopped carrots

- 1/4 cup chopped red onion

- 1/4 cup diced tofu

- 1 tablespoon olive oil

- 1/4 teaspoon dried thyme

- 1/4 teaspoon dried rosemary

- Salt and pepper to taste

Instructions:

1. Preheat oven to 400°F (200°C).

2. Drizzle olive oil over vegetables.

3. Toss to coat and arrange on a baking sheet.

4. Sprinkle with thyme and rosemary.

5. Bake for 15-20 minutes, or until vegetables are tender.

6. In a small skillet, cook tofu until browned.

7. Combine cooked quinoa, roasted vegetables, and tofu in a bowl.

8. Season with salt and pepper to taste.

Cook Time: 20-25 minutes | **Prep Time:** 15 minutes | **Portion Size:** 1 serving

Nutritional Facts per Meal (approximate):

Calories: 350-400

Protein: 20-25 grams

Carbohydrates: 35-40 grams

Fat: 15-20 grams

Potassium: Low

Diet Ideas:

1. For a vegetarian option, use a different type of tofu or tempeh.

2. For a low-fat option, use less olive oil.

3. For added flavor, sprinkle with sesame seeds or chopped scallions.

4. For a whole-grain option, use a different type of grain instead of quinoa.

Stuffed Bell Peppers with Ground Turkey

Short Description: A flavorful and satisfying dinner option that is low in potassium and packed with protein.

Ingredients:

- 2 large bell peppers

- 1 pound ground turkey

- 1/2 cup chopped onion

- 1/4 cup chopped celery

- 1/4 cup chopped red pepper

- 1 can (15 ounces) tomato sauce

- 1/4 cup grated Parmesan cheese

- Salt and pepper to taste

Instructions:

1. Preheat oven to 375°F (190°C).

2. Cut bell peppers in half lengthwise and remove seeds.

3. In a large skillet, cook ground turkey until browned. Drain any excess fat.

4. Add onion, celery, and red pepper to skillet and cook until softened.

5. Stir in tomato sauce, Parmesan cheese, salt, and pepper.

6. Stuff bell peppers with the turkey mixture.

7. Place stuffed bell peppers on a baking sheet and bake for 20-25 minutes, or until tender.

Cook Time: 30-35 minutes | **Prep Time:** 20 minutes | **Portion Size:** 2 servings

Nutritional Facts per Meal (approximate):

Calories: 350-400

Protein: 30-35 grams

Carbohydrates: 20-25 grams

Fat: 15-20 grams

Potassium: Low

Diet Ideas:

1. For a vegetarian option, substitute ground turkey with plant-based ground meat.

2. For a low-fat option, drain the fat from the ground turkey and use a low-fat tomato sauce.

3. For added flavor, sprinkle with crumbled feta cheese or a squeeze of lemon juice.

4. For a whole-grain option, serve with a side of brown rice or quinoa.

Vegetable Curry with Brown Rice

Short Description: A hearty and comforting dinner option that is low in potassium and packed with protein and nutrients.

Ingredients:

- 1 tablespoon olive oil

- 1 onion, chopped

- 1 carrot, chopped

- 1 celery stalk, chopped

- 1 can (15 ounces) coconut milk

- 1 tablespoon curry powder

- 1 teaspoon ground cumin

- 1/2 teaspoon ground turmeric

- Salt and pepper to taste

- 1 cup cooked brown rice

Instructions:

1. Heat olive oil in a large pot over medium heat.

2. Add onion, carrot, and celery, and cook until softened.

3. Stir in coconut milk, curry powder, cumin, turmeric, salt, and pepper.

4. Bring to a simmer and cook for 10-15 minutes, or until thickened.

5. Serve over cooked brown rice.

Cook Time: 30-35 minutes | **Prep Time:** 15 minutes | **Portion Size:** 1 serving

Nutritional Facts per Meal (approximate):

Calories: 350-400

Protein: 10-15 grams

Carbohydrates: 40-45 grams

Fat: 15-20 grams

Potassium: Low

Diet Ideas:

1. For a vegetarian option, use vegetable broth instead of coconut milk.

2. For a low-fat option, use light coconut milk or a reduced-fat dairy alternative.

3. For added flavor, sprinkle with chopped cilantro or fresh lime juice.

4. For a whole-grain option, use a different type of brown rice.

Grilled Salmon with Roasted Vegetables

Short Description: A healthy and flavorful dinner option that is low in potassium and packed with protein and nutrients.

Ingredients:

- 1 salmon fillet

- 1 bunch asparagus, trimmed

- 1/2 cup chopped broccoli florets

- 1/4 cup chopped red onion

- 1 tablespoon olive oil

- 1/4 teaspoon dried dill

- 1/4 teaspoon dried parsley

- Salt and pepper to taste

Instructions:

1. Preheat oven to 400°F (200°C).

2. Season salmon with salt and pepper.

3. Drizzle olive oil over vegetables.

4. Toss to coat and arrange on a baking sheet with salmon.

5. Sprinkle with dill and parsley.

6. Bake for 15-20 minutes, or until salmon is cooked through and vegetables are tender.

Cook Time: 15-20 minutes | **Prep Time:** 10 minutes | **Portion Size:** 1 serving

Nutritional Facts per Meal (approximate):

Calories: 350-400

Protein: 30-35 grams

Carbohydrates: 20-25 grams

Fat: 20-25 grams

Potassium: Low

Diet Ideas:

1. For a vegetarian option, substitute salmon with tofu or tempeh.

2. For a low-fat option, use less olive oil.

3. For added flavor, sprinkle with lemon zest or a squeeze of lemon juice.

4. For a whole-grain option, serve with a side of brown rice or quinoa.

PART 5: SIDE DISHES

Roasted Broccoli with Lemon and Garlic

Short Description: A simple and delicious side dish that is low in potassium and packed with nutrients.

Ingredients:

- 1 bunch broccoli, cut into florets
- 1 tablespoon olive oil
- 1 clove garlic, minced
- 1/2 lemon, juiced
- Salt and pepper to taste

Instructions:

1. Preheat oven to 400°F (200°C).
2. Toss broccoli with olive oil, garlic, lemon juice, salt, and pepper.
3. Spread broccoli on a baking sheet.
4. Roast for 15-20 minutes, or until tender and slightly browned.

Cook Time: 15-20 minutes | **Prep Time:** 5 minutes | **Portion Size:** 1 serving

Nutritional Facts per Meal (approximate):

Calories: 50-75

Protein: 3-5 grams

Carbohydrates: 5-7 grams

Fiber: 3-4 grams

Potassium: Low

Diet Ideas:

1. For a vegan option, use olive oil and lemon juice.

2. For a low-fat option, use less olive oil.

3. For added flavor, sprinkle with Parmesan cheese or red pepper flakes.

4. For a whole-grain option, serve with a side of brown rice or quinoa.

Steamed Green Beans with Butter

Short Description: A classic side dish that is low in potassium and easy to prepare.

Ingredients:

- 1 pound green beans, trimmed

- 1 tablespoon butter

- Salt and pepper to taste

Instructions:

1. Bring a pot of salted water to a boil.

2. Add green beans and cook for 3-5 minutes, or until tender-crisp.

3. Drain and return green beans to pot.

4. Stir in butter, salt, and pepper.

Cook Time: 5-7 minutes | **Prep Time:** 5 minutes | **Portion Size:** 1 serving

Nutritional Facts per Meal (approximate):

Calories: 50-75

Protein: 2-3 grams

Carbohydrates: 5-7 grams

Fiber: 2-3 grams

Potassium: Low

Diet Ideas:

1. For a vegan option, use olive oil or vegetable broth instead of butter.

2. For added flavor, sprinkle with grated Parmesan cheese or a squeeze of lemon juice.

3. For a whole-grain option, serve with a side of brown rice or quinoa.

Roasted Asparagus with Parmesan Cheese

Short Description: A flavorful and nutritious side dish that is low in potassium and packed with vitamins and minerals.

Ingredients:

- 1 bunch asparagus, trimmed
- 1 tablespoon olive oil
- 1/4 cup grated Parmesan cheese
- Salt and pepper to taste

Instructions:

1. Preheat oven to 400°F (200°C).
2. Toss asparagus with olive oil, salt, and pepper.
3. Spread asparagus on a baking sheet.
4. Roast for 10-15 minutes, or until tender-crisp.
5. Sprinkle with Parmesan cheese.

Cook Time: 10-15 minutes | **Prep Time:** 5 minutes | **Portion Size:** 1 serving

Nutritional Facts per Meal (approximate):

Calories: 50-75

Protein: 2-3 grams

Carbohydrates: 5-7 grams

Fiber: 2-3 grams

Potassium: Low

Diet Ideas:

1. For a vegan option, use olive oil and a plant-based Parmesan cheese substitute.

2. For a low-fat option, use less olive oil.

3. For added flavor, sprinkle with red pepper flakes or a squeeze of lemon juice.

4. For a whole-grain option, serve with a side of brown rice or quinoa.

Sautéed Spinach with Garlic

Short Description: A quick and easy side dish that is low in potassium and packed with nutrients.

Ingredients:

- 1 bunch spinach

- 1 clove garlic, minced

- 1 tablespoon olive oil

- Salt and pepper to taste

Instructions:

1. Heat olive oil in a large skillet over medium heat.

2. Add spinach and cook until wilted.

3. Stir in garlic and cook for 1 minute more.

4. Season with salt and pepper.

Cook Time: 5-7 minutes | **Prep Time:** 5 minutes | **Portion Size:** 1 serving

Nutritional Facts per Meal (approximate):

Calories: 50-75

Protein: 2-3 grams

Carbohydrates: 5-7 grams

Fiber: 2-3 grams

Potassium: Low

Diet Ideas:

1. For a vegan option, use olive oil.

2. For added flavor, sprinkle with Parmesan cheese or a squeeze of lemon juice.

3. For a whole-grain option, serve with a side of brown rice or quinoa.

Grilled Zucchini with Balsamic Glaze

Short Description: A flavorful and nutritious side dish that is low in potassium and packed with vitamins and minerals.

Ingredients:

- 1 medium zucchini, sliced
- 1 tablespoon olive oil
- 1 tablespoon balsamic vinegar
- 1 teaspoon honey
- Salt and pepper to taste

Instructions:

1. Preheat grill to medium heat.
2. Toss zucchini with olive oil, balsamic vinegar, honey, salt, and pepper.
3. Grill zucchini for 3-5 minutes per side, or until tender-crisp.

Cook Time: 10-15 minutes | **Prep Time:** 5 minutes | **Portion Size:** 1 serving

Nutritional Facts per Meal (approximate):

Calories: 50-75

Protein: 1-2 grams

Carbohydrates: 5-7 grams

Fiber: 2-3 grams

Potassium: Low

Diet Ideas:

1. For a vegan option, use olive oil, balsamic vinegar, and honey.

2. For a low-fat option, use less olive oil.

3. For added flavor, sprinkle with red pepper flakes or a squeeze of lemon juice.

4. For a whole-grain option, serve with a side of brown rice or quinoa.

Baked Sweet Potato Fries

Short Description: A healthy and delicious alternative to traditional french fries.

Ingredients:

- 1 large sweet potato, peeled and cut into fries

- 1 tablespoon olive oil

- 1/4 teaspoon paprika

- 1/4 teaspoon garlic powder

- Salt and pepper to taste

Instructions:

1. Preheat oven to 400°F (200°C).

2. Toss sweet potato fries with olive oil, paprika, garlic powder, salt, and pepper.

3. Spread fries on a baking sheet.

4. Bake for 20-25 minutes, or until golden brown and crispy.

Cook Time: 20-25 minutes | **Prep Time:** 10 minutes | **Portion Size:** 1 serving

Nutritional Facts per Meal (approximate):

Calories: 100-125

Protein: 2-3 grams

Carbohydrates: 20-25 grams

Fiber: 4-5 grams

Potassium: Low

Diet Ideas:

1. For a vegan option, use olive oil and spices.

2. For a low-fat option, use less olive oil or a non-stick baking sheet.

3. For added flavor, sprinkle with chili powder or a squeeze of lemon juice.

4. For a whole-grain option, serve with a side of brown rice or quinoa.

Quinoa Salad with Vegetables

Short Description: A nutritious and flavorful side dish that is low in potassium and packed with vitamins and minerals.

Ingredients:

- 1 cup cooked quinoa

- 1/2 cup chopped cucumber

- 1/4 cup chopped red onion

- 1/4 cup chopped red bell pepper

- 1/4 cup low-potassium salad dressing of your choice

- Salt and pepper to taste

Instructions:

1. In a large bowl, combine quinoa, cucumber, red onion, and red bell pepper.

2. Toss with salad dressing and season with salt and pepper.

Cook Time: None (if quinoa is pre-cooked) | **Prep Time:** 10 minutes | **Portion Size:** 1 serving

Nutritional Facts per Meal (approximate):

Calories: 200-250

Protein: 5-7 grams

Carbohydrates: 30-35 grams

Fiber: 3-4 grams

Potassium: Low

Diet Ideas:

1. For a vegan option, use a plant-based salad dressing.

2. For a low-fat option, use a light or vinaigrette-based salad dressing.

3. For added flavor, sprinkle with feta cheese or a squeeze of lemon juice.

4. For a whole-grain option, use a different type of quinoa.

Roasted Carrots with Rosemary

Short Description: A simple and delicious side dish that is low in potassium and packed with nutrients.

Ingredients:

*   1 pound carrots, peeled and cut into chunks

*   1 tablespoon olive oil

*   1 teaspoon dried rosemary

*   Salt and pepper to taste

Instructions:

1. Preheat oven to 400°F (200°C).

2. Toss carrots with olive oil, rosemary, salt, and pepper.

3. Spread carrots on a baking sheet.

4. Roast for 20-25 minutes, or until tender-crisp.

Cook Time: 20-25 minutes | **Prep Time:** 10 minutes | **Portion Size:** 1 serving

Nutritional Facts per Meal (approximate):

Calories: 100-125

Protein: 2-3 grams

Carbohydrates: 20-25 grams

Fiber: 3-4 grams

Potassium: Low

Diet Ideas:

1. For a vegan option, use olive oil and rosemary.

2. For a low-fat option, use less olive oil.

3. For added flavor, sprinkle with Parmesan cheese or a squeeze of lemon juice.

4. For a whole-grain option, serve with a side of brown rice or quinoa.

Steamed Cauliflower with Lemon and Dill

Short Description: A simple and nutritious side dish that is low in potassium and packed with vitamins and minerals.

Ingredients:

- 1 head cauliflower, cut into florets
- 1 tablespoon olive oil
- 1/2 lemon, juiced
- 1 teaspoon dried dill
- Salt and pepper to taste

Instructions:

1. Steam cauliflower until tender-crisp.
2. Toss with olive oil, lemon juice, dill, salt, and pepper.

Cook Time: 10-15 minutes | **Prep Time:** 5 minutes | **Portion Size:** 1 serving

Nutritional Facts per Meal (approximate):

Calories: 50-75

Protein: 2-3 grams

Carbohydrates: 5-7 grams

Fiber: 3-4 grams

Potassium: Low

Diet Ideas:

1. For a vegan option, use olive oil and lemon juice.

2. For added flavor, sprinkle with Parmesan cheese or red pepper flakes.

3. For a whole-grain option, serve with a side of brown rice or quinoa.

Sautéed Mushrooms with Garlic and Butter

Short Description: A flavorful and savory side dish that is low in potassium and packed with nutrients.

Ingredients:

- 1 pound mixed mushrooms, sliced

- 1 tablespoon butter

- 1 clove garlic, minced

- Salt and pepper to taste

Instructions:

1. Heat butter in a large skillet over medium heat.

2. Add mushrooms and sauté until browned and cooked through.

3. Stir in garlic and cook for 1 minute more.

4. Season with salt and pepper.

Cook Time: 10-15 minutes | **Prep Time:** 5 minutes | **Portion Size:** 1 serving

Nutritional Facts per Meal (approximate):

Calories: 100-125

Protein: 2-3 grams

Carbohydrates: 5-7 grams

Fiber: 2-3 grams

Potassium: Low

Diet Ideas:

1. For a vegan option, use olive oil instead of butter.

2. For added flavor, sprinkle with Parmesan cheese or a squeeze of lemon juice.

3. For a whole-grain option, serve with a side of brown rice or quinoa.

Roasted Brussels Sprouts with Balsamic Glaze

Short Description: A delicious and nutritious side dish that is low in potassium and packed with vitamins and minerals.

Ingredients:

- 1 pound Brussels sprouts, trimmed and halved
- 2 tablespoons olive oil
- 1/4 cup balsamic vinegar
- 1 tablespoon maple syrup
- 1/4 teaspoon dried thyme
- Salt and pepper to taste

Instructions:

1. Preheat oven to 400°F (200°C).
2. Toss Brussels sprouts with olive oil, balsamic vinegar, maple syrup, thyme, salt, and pepper.
3. Roast for 20-25 minutes, or until tender-crisp and slightly browned.

Cook Time: 20-25 minutes | **Prep Time:** 10 minutes | **Portion Size:** 1 serving

Nutritional Facts per Meal (approximate):

Calories: 100-125

Protein: 3-4 grams

Carbohydrates: 10-15 grams

Fiber: 4-5 grams

Potassium: Low

Diet Ideas:

- For a vegan option, use the recipe as is.
- For added flavor, sprinkle with Parmesan cheese or red pepper flakes.
- For a whole-grain option, serve with a side of brown rice or quinoa.

Apple Slices with Almond Butter

Short Description: A simple and satisfying snack that is low in potassium and packed with protein and fiber.

Ingredients:

- 1 apple, sliced

- 1 tablespoon almond butter

Instructions:

1. Spread almond butter on apple slices.

Prep Time: 5 minutes | **Portion Size:** 1 apple

Nutritional Facts per Meal (approximate):

Calories: 100-125

Protein: 5-7 grams

Carbohydrates: 20-25 grams

Fat: 5-7 grams

Potassium: Low

Diet Ideas:

1. For a vegan option, use plant-based almond butter.

2. For a nut-free option, use a different nut butter or a seed butter.

3. For added flavor, sprinkle with cinnamon or a drizzle of honey.

Greek Yogurt with Berries

Short Description: A refreshing and nutritious snack that is low in potassium and packed with protein.

Ingredients:

- 1/2 cup Greek yogurt

- 1/2 cup mixed berries (blueberries, strawberries, raspberries)

- Honey or maple syrup to taste

Instructions:

1. Combine Greek yogurt and berries in a bowl.

2. Drizzle with honey or maple syrup to taste.

Prep Time: 5 minutes | **Portion Size:** 1 serving

Nutritional Facts per Meal (approximate):

Calories: 150-200

Protein: 15-20 grams

Carbohydrates: 20-25 grams

Fat: 5-10 grams

Potassium: Low

Diet Ideas:

1. For a vegan option, use plant-based Greek yogurt.

2. For a nut-free option, omit nuts.

3. For added protein, top with a scoop of protein powder.

4. For a thicker parfait, add a spoonful of chia seeds.

Cucumber Sticks with Hummus

Short Description: A healthy and satisfying snack that is low in potassium and packed with protein.

Ingredients:

- 1 cucumber, sliced into sticks

- 1/4 cup hummus

Instructions:

1. Spread hummus on cucumber sticks.

Prep Time: 5 minutes | **Portion Size:** 1 cucumber

Nutritional Facts per Meal (approximate):

Calories: 100-125

Protein: 5-7 grams

Carbohydrates: 10-15 grams

Fat: 5-7 grams

Potassium: Low

Diet Ideas:

1. For a vegan option, use plant-based hummus.

2. For a low-fat option, use a light or reduced-fat hummus.

3. For added flavor, sprinkle with paprika or a squeeze of lemon juice.

4. For a whole-grain option, serve with whole-grain crackers.

Carrot Sticks with Low-Potassium Ranch Dressing

Short Description: A classic and satisfying snack that is low in potassium and packed with nutrients.

Ingredients:

- 1 large carrot, cut into sticks
- 1/4 cup low-potassium ranch dressing

Instructions:

1. Dip carrot sticks into ranch dressing.

Prep Time: 5 minutes | **Portion Size:** 1 carrot

Nutritional Facts per Meal (approximate):

Calories: 50-75

Protein: 1-2 grams

Carbohydrates: 10-15 grams

Fiber: 2-3 grams

Potassium: Low

Diet Ideas:

1. For a vegan option, use a plant-based ranch dressing.

2. For a low-fat option, use a light or reduced-fat ranch dressing.

3. For added flavor, sprinkle with paprika or a squeeze of lemon juice.

4. For a whole-grain option, serve with whole-grain crackers.

Hard-Boiled Eggs

Short Description: A simple and protein-packed snack that is low in potassium and easy to prepare.

Ingredients:

- 2 large eggs

Instructions:

1. Place eggs in a saucepan and cover with cold water.

2. Bring to a boil, then reduce heat and simmer for 10-12 minutes.

3. Drain the water and run cold water over the eggs to cool them down.

4. Peel the eggs and serve.

Cook Time: 15-20 minutes | **Prep Time:** 5 minutes | **Portion Size:** 2 eggs

Nutritional Facts per Meal (approximate):

Calories: 150-200

Protein: 15-20 grams

Carbohydrates: 1-2 grams

Fat: 10-12 grams

Potassium: Low

Diet Ideas:

1. For a whole-grain option, serve with whole-grain toast or crackers.

2. For added flavor, sprinkle with paprika or a squeeze of lemon juice.

Celery Sticks with Peanut Butter

Short Description: A crunchy and satisfying snack that is low in potassium and packed with protein.

Ingredients:

- 1 celery stalk, cut into sticks

- 1/4 cup peanut butter

Instructions:

1. Spread peanut butter on celery sticks.

Prep Time: 5 minutes | **Portion Size:** 1 celery stalk

Nutritional Facts per Meal (approximate):

Calories: 100-125

Protein: 5-7 grams

Carbohydrates: 5-7 grams

Fat: 8-10 grams

Potassium: Low

Diet Ideas:

1. For a vegan option, use plant-based peanut butter.

2. For a nut-free option, use a different nut butter or a seed butter.

3. For added flavor, sprinkle with cinnamon or a drizzle of honey.

Low-Potassium Trail Mix

Short Description: A healthy and satisfying snack that is low in potassium and packed with protein and fiber.

Ingredients:

- 1/2 cup unsalted almonds

- 1/4 cup sunflower seeds

- 1/4 cup dried apricots

- 1/4 cup dried cranberries

- 1/4 cup raisins

- 1/4 cup dark chocolate chips

Instructions:

Combine all ingredients in a bowl and mix well.

Prep Time: 5 minutes | **Portion Size:** 1/4 cup

Nutritional Facts per Meal (approximate):

Calories: 200-250

Protein: 7-10 grams

Carbohydrates: 25-30 grams

Fat: 15-20 grams

Potassium: Low

Diet Ideas:

1. For a vegan option, use plant-based dark chocolate chips.

2. For a nut-free option, omit almonds and sunflower seeds.

3. For added flavor, sprinkle with cinnamon or a drizzle of honey.

4. For a whole-grain option, add a handful of whole-grain cereal.

Whole-Grain Crackers with Cheese

Short Description: A classic and satisfying snack that is low in potassium and packed with protein.

Ingredients:

- 2 whole-grain crackers

- 1 slice low-sodium cheese

Instructions:

1. Place cheese on top of crackers.

Prep Time: 5 minutes | **Portion Size:** 2 crackers

Nutritional Facts per Meal (approximate):

Calories: 100-125

Protein: 5-7 grams

Carbohydrates: 20-25 grams

Fat: 5-7 grams

Potassium: Low

Diet Ideas:

1. For a vegan option, use plant-based cheese.

2. For a low-fat option, use a light or reduced-fat cheese.

3. For added flavor, sprinkle with paprika or a squeeze of lemon juice.

4. For a whole-grain option, use thicker whole-grain crackers.

Fruit Smoothie

Short Description: A refreshing and nutritious snack that is low in potassium and packed with vitamins and minerals.

Ingredients:

- 1 cup mixed berries (blueberries, strawberries, raspberries)

- 1 banana, peeled and sliced

- 1 cup almond milk

- 1 tablespoon honey (optional)

Instructions:

1. Combine all ingredients in a blender.

2. Blend until smooth.

3. Pour into a glass and enjoy immediately.

Cook Time: 5 minutes | **Prep Time:** 5 minutes | **Portion Size:** 1 serving

Nutritional Facts per Meal (approximate):

Calories: 200-250

Protein: 7-10 grams

Carbohydrates: 30-35 grams

Fiber: 5-7 grams

Potassium: Low

Diet Ideas:

1. For a vegan option, use plant-based almond milk and honey.

2. For a nut-free option, use a different type of milk, such as oat or soy.

3. For added protein, add a scoop of protein powder.

4. For a thicker smoothie, add more chia seeds.

Cottage Cheese with Fruit

Short Description: A simple and nutritious snack that is low in potassium and packed with protein.

Ingredients:

- 1/2 cup cottage cheese
- 1/2 cup mixed berries (blueberries, strawberries, raspberries)
- Honey or maple syrup to taste

Instructions:

1. Combine cottage cheese and berries in a bowl.
2. Drizzle with honey or maple syrup to taste.

Prep Time: 5 minutes | **Portion Size:** 1 serving

Nutritional Facts per Meal (approximate):

Calories: 150-200

Protein: 15-20 grams

Carbohydrates: 20-25 grams

Fat: 5-10 grams

Potassium: Low

Diet Ideas:

1. For a vegan option, use plant-based cottage cheese.

2. For a nut-free option, omit nuts.

3. For added protein, top with a scoop of protein powder.

4. For a thicker parfait, add a spoonful of chia seeds.

Additional Snack Tips

*   **Plan ahead:** Prepare snacks in advance to avoid reaching for unhealthy options when you're hungry.

*   **Keep healthy snacks on hand:** Stock your fridge and pantry with low-potassium snacks like fruits, vegetables, nuts, and yogurt.

*   **Mindful eating:** Pay attention to your hunger cues and eat when you're truly hungry.

*   **Don't skip meals:** Eating regular meals can help prevent overeating and snacking on unhealthy foods.

*   **Enjoy your snacks:** Snacks should be a pleasurable experience. Choose foods that you enjoy and that satisfy your cravings.

Baked Apple with Cinnamon and Nutmeg

Short Description: A sweet and comforting dessert that is low in potassium and packed with fiber.

Ingredients:

- 1 large apple

- 1 tablespoon brown sugar (optional)

- 1/4 teaspoon ground cinnamon

- 1/4 teaspoon ground nutmeg

- 1 tablespoon butter

Instructions:

1. Preheat oven to 375°F (190°C).

2. Cut apple in half and remove core.

3. Fill the cavity with brown sugar (if using), cinnamon, and nutmeg.

4. Place apple halves on a baking sheet and top with butter.

5. Bake for 20-25 minutes, or until tender.

Cook Time: 20-25 minutes | **Prep Time:** 10 minutes | **Portion Size:** 1 serving

Nutritional Facts per Meal (approximate):

Calories: 150-200

Protein: 1-2 grams

Carbohydrates: 30-35 grams

Fiber: 5-7 grams

Potassium: Low

Diet Ideas:

1. For a vegan option, use plant-based butter.

2. For a low-sugar option, omit brown sugar.

3. For added flavor, sprinkle with a pinch of nutmeg or a drizzle of maple syrup.

Greek Yogurt Parfait with Berries and Granola

Short Description: A refreshing and nutritious dessert that is low in potassium and packed with protein.

Ingredients:

- 1/2 cup Greek yogurt

- 1/2 cup mixed berries (blueberries, strawberries, raspberries)

- 1/4 cup granola (low-potassium option)

- Honey or maple syrup to taste

Instructions:

1. In a glass or bowl, layer the yogurt, berries, and granola.

2. Drizzle with honey or maple syrup to taste.

Prep Time: 5 minutes | **Portion Size:** 1 serving

Nutritional Facts per Meal (approximate):

Calories: 200-250

Protein: 15-20 grams

Carbohydrates: 30-35 grams

Fat: 5-10 grams

Potassium: Low

Diet Ideas:

1. For a vegan option, use plant-based yogurt and granola.

2. For a nut-free option, choose a granola without nuts.

3. For added protein, top with a scoop of protein powder.

4. For a thicker parfait, add a spoonful of chia seeds.

Fruit Salad with Low-Potassium Dressing

Short Description: A simple and refreshing dessert that is low in potassium and packed with nutrients.

Ingredients:

- 2 cups mixed fruits (berries, apples, grapes)
- 1/4 cup low-potassium salad dressing of your choice

Instructions:

1. In a bowl, combine fruits and salad dressing.
2. Toss to coat.

Prep Time: 5 minutes | **Portion Size:** 1 serving

Nutritional Facts per Meal (approximate):

Calories: 150-200

Protein: 1-2 grams

Carbohydrates: 30-35 grams

Fiber: 4-5 grams

Potassium: Low

Diet Ideas:

1. For a vegan option, use a plant-based salad dressing.

2. For added flavor, sprinkle with a pinch of cinnamon or a drizzle of honey.

3. For a whole-grain option, serve with a side of whole-grain crackers or bread.

Chia Seed Pudding with Fruit and Nuts

Short Description: A creamy and nutritious dessert that is low in potassium and packed with fiber.

Ingredients:

- 1/4 cup chia seeds

- 1 cup low-potassium milk (almond, oat, or soy)

- 1/4 teaspoon vanilla extract

- Sweetener to taste (stevia, monk fruit extract, or honey)

- 1/2 cup mixed berries (blueberries, strawberries, raspberries)

- 1 tablespoon chopped nuts (almonds, walnuts, pecans)

Instructions:

1. In a small bowl, combine chia seeds, milk, vanilla extract, and sweetener.

2. Stir well and let sit for at least 30 minutes, or until thickened.

3. Stir in berries and nuts.

Prep Time: 30 minutes (plus chilling time) | **Portion Size:** 1 serving

Nutritional Facts per Meal (approximate):

Calories: 200-250

Protein: 5-7 grams

Carbohydrates: 30-35 grams

Fiber: 5-7 grams

Potassium: Low

Diet Ideas:

1. For a vegan option, use plant-based milk and sweetener.

2. For a nut-free option, omit nuts.

3. For added protein, top with a scoop of protein powder.

4. For a thicker pudding, add more chia seeds.

Frozen Berries with a Drizzle of Honey

Short Description: A simple and refreshing dessert that is low in potassium and packed with nutrients.

Ingredients:

- 1 cup mixed berries (blueberries, strawberries, raspberries)

- 1 tablespoon honey

Instructions:

1. Freeze berries until solid.

2. Serve with a drizzle of honey.

Prep Time: 5 minutes | **Portion Size:** 1 serving

Nutritional Facts per Meal (approximate):

Calories: 100-125

Protein: 1-2 grams

Carbohydrates: 20-25 grams

Fiber: 4-5 grams

Potassium: Low

Diet Ideas:

1. For a vegan option, use plant-based honey.

2. For added flavor, sprinkle with a pinch of cinnamon or a squeeze of lemon juice.

Chocolate Mousse Made with Avocado

Short Description: A decadent and creamy dessert that is low in potassium and packed with healthy fats.

Ingredients:

- 1 avocado, mashed

- 1/4 cup cocoa powder

- 1/4 cup maple syrup

- 1/4 cup almond milk

- 1/4 teaspoon vanilla extract

- Pinch of salt

Instructions:

1. In a blender, combine avocado, cocoa powder, maple syrup, almond milk, vanilla extract, and salt.

2. Blend until smooth and creamy.

Prep Time: 5 minutes | **Portion Size:** 1 serving

Nutritional Facts per Meal (approximate):

Calories: 200-250

Protein: 2-3 grams

Carbohydrates: 20-25 grams

Fat: 15-20 grams

Potassium: Low

Diet Ideas:

1. For a vegan option, use plant-based almond milk and maple syrup.

2. For a nut-free option, use a different type of milk, such as oat or soy.

3. For added flavor, sprinkle with chocolate shavings or a mint leaf.

Baked Pears with Cinnamon and Honey

Short Description: A sweet and comforting dessert that is low in potassium and packed with fiber.

Ingredients:

- 2 pears, peeled and cored

- 1 tablespoon honey

- 1/4 teaspoon ground cinnamon

- 1/4 teaspoon ground nutmeg

Instructions:

1. Preheat oven to 375°F (190°C).

2. Place pears in a baking dish.

3. Drizzle with honey and sprinkle with cinnamon and nutmeg.

4. Bake for 20-25 minutes, or until tender.

Cook Time: 20-25 minutes | **Prep Time:** 5 minutes | **Portion Size:** 1 serving

Nutritional Facts per Meal (approximate):

Calories: 150-200

Protein: 1-2 grams

Carbohydrates: 30-35 grams

Fiber: 5-7 grams

Potassium: Low

Diet Ideas:

1. For a vegan option, use plant-based honey.

2. For added flavor, sprinkle with a pinch of ginger or a drizzle of maple syrup.

Angel Food Cake with Whipped Cream and Berries

Short Description: A light and fluffy dessert that is low in potassium and perfect for special occasions.

Ingredients:

*   1 angel food cake

- 1 cup whipped cream

- 1 cup mixed berries (blueberries, strawberries, raspberries)

Instructions:

1. Slice angel food cake into desired servings.

2. Top with whipped cream and berries.

Prep Time: 5 minutes | **Portion Size:** 1 serving

Nutritional Facts per Meal (approximate):

Calories: 250-300

Protein: 2-3 grams

Carbohydrates: 40-45 grams

Fat: 10-15 grams

Potassium: Low

Diet Ideas:

1. For a vegan option, use plant-based whipped cream.

2. For added flavor, sprinkle with a dusting of powdered sugar or a drizzle of chocolate syrup.

Homemade Fruit Sorbet

Short Description: A refreshing and healthy dessert that is low in potassium and packed with nutrients.

Ingredients:

- 2 cups mixed fruits (berries, mango, pineapple)
- 1/4 cup water
- 1/4 cup honey (optional)

Instructions:

1. Combine fruits, water, and honey (if using) in a blender.
2. Blend until smooth.
3. Pour mixture into a freezer-safe container and freeze for at least 2 hours, or until firm.
4. Break up frozen sorbet with a fork before serving.

Prep Time: 10 minutes | **Portion Size:** 1 serving

Nutritional Facts per Meal (approximate):

Calories: 150-200

Protein: 1-2 grams

Carbohydrates: 30-35 grams

Fiber: 4-5 grams

Potassium: Low

Diet Ideas:

1. For a vegan option, use plant-based honey.

2. For added flavor, sprinkle with a pinch of cinnamon or a squeeze of lemon juice.

Low-Potassium Ice Cream Alternative with Fruit

Short Description: A creamy and indulgent dessert that is low in potassium and perfect for a sweet treat.

Ingredients:

- 1 banana, frozen

- 1/2 cup Greek yogurt

- 1/4 cup almond milk

- 1/4 cup mixed berries (blueberries, strawberries, raspberries)

- Sweetener to taste (stevia, monk fruit extract, or honey)

Instructions:

1. Combine all ingredients in a blender and blend until smooth.

2. Serve immediately.

Prep Time: 5 minutes | **Portion Size:** 1 serving

Nutritional Facts per Meal (approximate):

Calories: 200-250

Protein: 15-20 grams

Carbohydrates: 30-35 grams

Fat: 5-10 grams

Potassium: Low

Diet Ideas:

1. For a vegan option, use plant-based Greek yogurt and almond milk.

2. For a nut-free option, use a different type of milk, such as oat or soy.

3. For added flavor, sprinkle with chocolate shavings or a mint leaf.

Additional Dessert Tips

- **Indulge in moderation:** Desserts can be enjoyed in moderation as part of a balanced diet.

- **Focus on quality ingredients:** Choose fresh, whole foods to create nutritious and delicious desserts.

- **Experiment with flavors:** Don't be afraid to try new ingredients and combinations.

- **Share with loved ones:** Desserts can be a great way to connect with friends and family.

- **Enjoy the moment:** Savoring a sweet treat can be a delightful way to end a meal or celebrate a special occasion.

PART 8: SPECIAL CONSIDERATIONS

Dietary Restrictions

This cookbook can easily be adapted to accommodate seniors with gluten-free or dairy-free dietary restrictions. **Here are some tips:**

Gluten-Free:

Substitute flours: Use gluten-free flours like almond flour, coconut flour, or oat flour in recipes that call for wheat flour.

Choose gluten-free grains: Opt for gluten-free grains like quinoa, brown rice, and amaranth.

Read labels carefully: Ensure all ingredients are gluten-free, especially in processed foods.

Dairy-Free:

Use dairy alternatives: Substitute dairy products with plant-based alternatives like almond milk, soy milk, coconut milk, and dairy-free yogurt.

Look for dairy-free cheese: Many dairy-free cheese options are now available, including mozzarella, cheddar, and Parmesan.

Choose dairy-free ingredients: Ensure all ingredients, including sauces and dressings, are dairy-free.

Additional Tips:

Communicate with your healthcare provider: Discuss your dietary restrictions with your healthcare provider to ensure you're meeting your nutritional needs.

Read labels carefully: Always check food labels for allergens, including gluten and dairy.

Experiment with different ingredients: Don't be afraid to try new gluten-free or dairy-free alternatives to find what you enjoy.

Consider a registered dietitian: A registered dietitian can provide personalized guidance and help you create a meal plan that meets your dietary needs.

By following these tips, you can easily adapt the recipes in "The Complete Low Potassium Cookbook for Seniors" to accommodate gluten-free or dairy-free diets.

Tips for Eating Out Safely

Eating out can be challenging when following a low-potassium diet, but it's possible with a little planning and preparation. **The following advice can assist you in navigating restaurant menus and selecting healthful options:**

Before You Go:

Research restaurants: Look for restaurants that offer healthy options or have online menus you can review in advance.

Ask about ingredients: Contact the restaurant ahead of time to inquire about the potassium content of specific dishes or ingredients.

Plan your meal: Decide what you'll order before you arrive to avoid making impulsive choices.

At the Restaurant:

Start with a salad or appetizer: Many restaurants offer low-potassium options like salads or appetizers that can be a healthy start to your meal.

Choose grilled or baked options: Opt for grilled, baked, or steamed dishes over fried options, as these are generally lower in potassium and fat.

Avoid sauces and gravies: Sauces and gravies can be high in potassium and sodium. Ask for them on the side or request a sauce made with herbs and spices instead.

Watch out for hidden potassium: Be aware of hidden sources of potassium, such as added salt or MSG.

Portion control: To prevent overindulging, pay attention to portion proportions.

When Ordering:

Ask for modifications: Don't hesitate to ask the server if modifications can be made to a dish to make it lower in potassium. For example, you might ask for a side of vegetables instead of potatoes or rice.

Be specific: Clearly communicate your dietary needs to the server, including your low-potassium requirements.

Check the menu carefully: Look for dishes that are naturally low in potassium, such as grilled fish, chicken, or lean meats.

Additional Tips:

Bring your own snacks: If you're unsure about the options available at the restaurant, bring your own low-potassium snacks to tide you over.

Don't be afraid to ask questions: If you're unsure about the potassium content of a dish, don't hesitate to ask the server or chef.

Enjoy yourself: Eating out should be a pleasurable experience. Don't stress too much about following a strict diet. Just make healthy choices and savor your meal.

By following these tips, you can enjoy eating out while staying on track with your low-potassium diet.

Tips for Meal Prep and Storage

Meal prep can be a valuable tool for managing a low-potassium diet. By preparing meals and snacks in advance, you can save time, reduce stress, and ensure you have healthy options readily available. Here are some pointers for preparing and storing meals:

1. Plan Your Meals:

Create a weekly meal plan: This will help you stay organized and ensure you have a variety of low-potassium meals throughout the week.

Consider your schedule: Plan your meals around your daily activities and commitments.

Involve family or roommates: If you live with others, involve them in the meal planning process to ensure everyone's dietary needs are met.

2. Stock Your Pantry:

Stock your pantry with low-potassium staples: This includes whole grains, legumes, canned vegetables, and spices.

Keep a variety of ingredients on hand: This will allow you to create different meals throughout the week.

3. Prepare Ingredients in Advance:

Wash and chop vegetables, cook grains, and prepare protein sources in advance.

Store these ingredients in the refrigerator or freezer for easy use throughout the week.

4. Cook in Batches:

Cook larger quantities of food at once and portion it out into individual servings.

You'll save time and effort by doing this during the week.

5. Store Food Properly:

Store cooked foods in airtight containers in the refrigerator or freezer.

Label containers with the date and contents.

Follow recommended storage guidelines for each type of food.

6. Freeze Leftovers:

Freeze any leftover food for a later time

You can cut down on food waste and save money by doing this.

7. Create Grab-and-Go Snacks:

Prepare healthy snacks in advance, such as cut-up fruits and vegetables, trail mix, or hard-boiled eggs.

Store these snacks in the refrigerator or freezer for easy access.

8. Consider Meal Delivery Services:

If you're short on time or find meal prep challenging, consider using a meal delivery service that specializes in low-potassium meals.

By following these tips, you can make meal prep a breeze and simplify your low-potassium diet.

APPENDIX

The Importance of Potassium Content in Common Foods

Potassium is a vital mineral for the proper functioning of our bodies. It helps regulate blood pressure, heart rhythm, and muscle contractions. However, for individuals with certain health conditions, such as kidney disease or high blood pressure, excessive potassium intake can be harmful.

Understanding the potassium content of common foods is crucial for:

Managing hyperkalemia: Individuals with hyperkalemia, a condition where there is an excess of potassium in the blood, need to carefully monitor their potassium intake. By identifying and limiting high-potassium foods, they can help maintain healthy potassium levels.

Protecting kidney health: High potassium levels can strain the kidneys, leading to kidney damage or failure. By consuming foods low in potassium, individuals with kidney disease can help protect their kidneys.

Maintaining overall health: A balanced potassium intake is essential for overall health and well-being. Consuming a variety of foods that are low in potassium can help ensure you meet your nutritional needs while avoiding excessive intake.

It's important to note that:

Individual needs vary: The amount of potassium you can safely consume may depend on your specific health condition and medical advice.

Not all low-potassium foods are created equal: While some foods are naturally low in potassium, others may contain added potassium or be processed in ways that increase their potassium content.

By being aware of the potassium content in common foods and making informed choices, you can help manage your potassium intake and maintain optimal health.

Resources for Further Learning

Here are some reliable resources for further learning about hyperkalemia and kidney health:

Organizations:

- **National Kidney Foundation**
- **American Kidney Fund**
- **Chronic Kidney Disease Foundation**

Online Resources:

- **National Institutes of Health (NIH)**
- **Mayo Clinic**

- **Cleveland Clinic Health Essentials**

Books:

- **"The Complete Low Potassium Cookbook for Seniors"** by [Culinary Quill]
- **"The Kidney Diet: A Comprehensive Guide"** by Alan S. Nissenson and Karen E. Weinman
- **"The Mayo Clinic Diet Cookbook: Low-Sodium, Low-Potassium Edition"** by Mayo Clinic Staff

Medical Professionals:

- **Registered dietitian:** A registered dietitian can provide personalized guidance on creating a low-potassium diet.
- **Nephrologist:** A nephrologist is a medical professional who focuses on kidney disorders. They can offer valuable advice and treatment options for hyperkalemia.

By exploring these resources, you can gain a deeper understanding of hyperkalemia, kidney health, and the role of diet in managing these conditions.

Glossary of Terms

- **Hyperkalemia:** A medical condition where there is an excess of potassium in the blood.

- **Potassium:** A mineral essential for the proper functioning of the body, but excessive intake can be harmful for individuals with certain health conditions.

- **Low-potassium diet:** A dietary plan that limits the intake of potassium-rich foods.

- **Renal diet:** A specialized diet often recommended for individuals with kidney disease, which includes restrictions on potassium, sodium, phosphorus, and protein.

- **Potassium-rich foods:** Foods that contain high levels of potassium, such as bananas, potatoes, spinach, and avocados.

- **Low-potassium foods:** Foods that are naturally low in potassium, such as apples, berries, carrots, and lean proteins.

- **Potassium substitutes:** Salt substitutes that are low in potassium and can be used to enhance flavor without increasing potassium intake.

- **Meal planning:** The process of planning and preparing meals in advance to ensure they meet specific dietary needs, such as a low-potassium diet.

- **Food labels:** The nutritional information provided on food packaging, which includes information on potassium content.

- **Registered dietitian:** A healthcare professional who specializes in nutrition and can provide personalized guidance on creating a low-potassium diet.

- **Nephrologist:** A doctor who specializes in kidney diseases and can offer advice on managing hyperkalemia and creating a suitable diet.

- **Potassium content:** The amount of potassium present in a particular food.

- **Dietary restrictions:** Limitations on certain foods or nutrients, such as a low-potassium diet.

Understanding these key terms will help you navigate a low-potassium diet and make informed choices about the foods you eat.

BONUS: BALANCED MEAL PLAN

Tips for Satisfying Meal Plan

A balanced and satisfying low-potassium meal plan is essential for managing hyperkalemia and improving kidney health.

Here are some tips to help you create such a plan:

1. Consult a Healthcare Professional:

See a trained dietician or other healthcare specialist before making any big dietary changes. They can offer tailored advice depending on your particular requirements and health issues.

2. Understand Your Potassium Limits:

Work with your healthcare provider to determine your daily potassium intake limit. This will help you plan your meals accordingly.

3. Prioritize Low-Potassium Foods:

Focus on incorporating a variety of low-potassium fruits, vegetables, lean proteins, whole grains, and dairy alternatives into your meals.

Use the guidelines provided in the previous response to identify high-potassium foods and limit your intake.

4. Create a Meal Plan:

Plan your meals and snacks in advance to ensure you meet your nutritional needs while staying within your potassium limits.

Consider using a food diary or tracking app to monitor your potassium intake.

5. Balance Your Meals:

A balanced meal should contain healthy fats, carbs, and a source of protein. For example, you could have grilled chicken with roasted vegetables and brown rice for dinner.

6. Be Mindful of Hidden Potassium:

Be aware of hidden sources of potassium in processed foods, such as canned soups, canned vegetables, and processed meats.

Carefully read food labels, and if possible, select low-potassium products.

7. Experiment with Flavors:

Don't be afraid to experiment with different flavors and seasonings to keep your meals interesting and enjoyable.

Herbs, spices, and citrus can add flavor to your dishes without adding excess potassium.

8. Practice Portion Control:

Take care with portion sizes to prevent taking excessive amounts of potassium.

Use measuring cups and spoons to help control your intake.

9. Stay Hydrated:

Drinking plenty of fluids is essential for overall health, even when following a low-potassium diet. Water is a great option, but you can also enjoy other low-potassium beverages like unsweetened tea or herbal tea.

10. Never Be Afraid to Request Assistance:

If you're struggling to create a low-potassium meal plan or follow your dietary restrictions, don't hesitate to reach out to a registered dietitian or healthcare provider for support.

By following these tips, you can create a balanced and satisfying low-potassium meal plan that helps you manage hyperkalemia and improve your overall health.

30-Day Meal Plan

Week 1

- Day 1

  - **Breakfast:** Oatmeal with berries and nuts

  - **Lunch:** Chicken Taco Bowls

- **Dinner:** Baked chicken with roasted vegetables

- **Snack:** Apple slices with almond butter

- Day 2

  - **Breakfast:** Scrambled eggs with spinach and avocado

  - **Lunch:** Corn Fritters

  - **Dinner:** Salmon with roasted asparagus and quinoa

  - **Snack:** Greek yogurt with berries

- Day 3

  - **Breakfast:** Rice Pudding with Cinnamon

  - **Lunch:** Tuna salad sandwich on whole-grain bread

  - **Dinner:** Beef stir-fry with brown rice

  - **Snack:** Cucumber sticks with hummus

- Day 4

  - **Breakfast:** Smoothie with spinach, banana, and almond milk

  - **Lunch:** Vegetable Frittata

  - **Dinner:** Lentil soup with whole-grain bread

  - **Snack:** Carrot sticks with ranch dressing (low-potassium version)

- Day 5

- **Breakfast:** Whole-grain toast with avocado and a fried egg

- **Lunch:** Chicken salad sandwich on whole-grain bread

- **Dinner:** Grilled chicken with roasted vegetables

- **Snack:** Hard-boiled eggs

- Day 6

   - **Breakfast:** Cottage cheese with fruit and nuts

   - **Lunch:** Tuna Pasta Salad

   - **Dinner:** Quinoa bowl with roasted vegetables and tofu

   - **Snack:** Celery sticks with peanut butter

- Day 7

   - **Breakfast:** Pancakes made with almond flour

   - **Lunch:** Vegetable wrap with hummus

   - **Dinner:** Stuffed bell peppers with ground turkey

   - **Snack:** Trail mix (low-potassium version)

Week 2

- Day 8

   - **Breakfast:** Fruit and Yogurt Parfait

   - **Lunch:** Leftovers from dinner

   - **Dinner:** Vegetable curry with brown rice

- **Snack:** Whole-grain crackers with cheese

- Day 9

    - **Breakfast:** Hard-boiled eggs with whole-grain toast

    - **Lunch:** Salad with grilled chicken and low-potassium dressing

    - **Dinner:** Grilled salmon with roasted vegetables

    - **Snack:** Fruit smoothie

- Day 10

    - **Breakfast:** Whole-grain waffles with fruit and syrup

    - **Lunch:** Leftover pasta with tomato sauce and vegetables

    - **Dinner:** Baked chicken with roasted vegetables

    - **Snack:** Cottage cheese with fruit

- Day 11

    - **Breakfast:** Oatmeal with berries and nuts

    - **Lunch:** Chicken Taco Bowls

    - **Dinner:** Salmon with roasted asparagus and quinoa

    - **Snack:** Greek yogurt with berries

- Day 12

    - **Breakfast:** Scrambled eggs with spinach and avocado

- **Lunch:** Corn Fritters

- **Dinner:** Beef stir-fry with brown rice

- **Snack:** Cucumber sticks with hummus

- Day 13

  - **Breakfast:** Rice Pudding with Cinnamon

  - **Lunch:** Tuna salad sandwich on whole-grain bread

  - **Dinner:** Lentil soup with whole-grain bread

  - **Snack:** Carrot sticks with ranch dressing (low-potassium version)

- Day 14

  - **Breakfast:** Smoothie with spinach, banana, and almond milk

  - **Lunch:** Vegetable Frittata

  - **Dinner:** Grilled chicken with roasted vegetables

  - **Snack:** Hard-boiled eggs

Week 3

- Day 15

  - **Breakfast:** Savory Spinach and Cheese Muffins

  - **Lunch:** Spicy Vegetable Lo Mein

  - **Dinner:** Herb-Roasted Chicken Thighs

  - **Snack:** Homemade Hummus with Veggie Sticks

- Day 16

  - **Breakfast:** Banana Oatmeal Pancakes

  - **Lunch:** Quinoa Salad with Roasted Vegetables

  - **Dinner:** Stuffed Bell Peppers with Ground Turkey

  - **Snack:** Baked Sweet Potato Chips

- Day 17

  - **Breakfast:** Chia Seed Pudding with Almond Milk

  - **Lunch:** Chicken Caesar Wraps

  - **Dinner:** Vegetable Stir-Fry with Tofu

  - **Snack:** Fruit Salad with Honey Drizzle

- Day 18

  - **Breakfast:** Cottage Cheese Bowl with Pineapple

  - **Lunch:** Mediterranean Couscous Salad

  - **Dinner:** Baked Salmon with Dill Sauce

  - **Snack:** Rice Cakes with Almond Butter

- Day 19

  - **Breakfast:** Egg Muffins with Bell Peppers and Cheese

  - **Lunch:** Vegetable Soup with Whole-Grain Bread

  - **Dinner:** Zucchini Noodles with Marinara Sauce

- **Snack:** Yogurt Parfait with Granola

- Day 20

  - **Breakfast:** Smoothie Bowl topped with Berries

  - **Lunch:** Chicken Quesadilla on Whole Wheat Tortilla

  - **Dinner:** Lentil Stew with Carrots and Celery

  - **Snack:** Popcorn Seasoned with Herbs

- Day 21

  - **Breakfast:** Peach Yogurt Smoothie

  - **Lunch:** Turkey Lettuce Wraps

  - **Dinner:** Stuffed Acorn Squash

  - **Snack:** Carrot Sticks with Low-Fat Ranch Dip

Week 4

- Day 22

  - **Breakfast:** Almond Butter Banana Toast

  - **Lunch:** Mediterranean Quinoa Bowl

  - **Dinner:** Herb-Crusted Tilapia

  - **Snack:** Cucumber Rounds with Cream Cheese

- Day 23

- **Breakfast:** Berry Smoothie Bowl

- **Lunch:** Turkey and Spinach Wrap

- **Dinner:** Stuffed Zucchini Boats

- **Snack:** Baked Apple Slices

- Day 24

   - **Breakfast:** Egg and Veggie Breakfast Burrito

   - **Lunch:** Chickpea Salad

   - **Dinner:** Grilled Chicken Skewers

   - **Snack:** Trail Mix (Low-Potassium Version)

- Day 25

   - **Breakfast:** Peach Chia Seed Pudding

   - **Lunch:** Vegetable Fried Rice (Low-Potassium)

   - **Dinner:** Baked Lemon Garlic Shrimp

   - **Snack:** Celery Sticks with Cream Cheese

- Day 26

   - **Breakfast:** Cottage Cheese Bowl with Berries

   - **Lunch:** Pasta Primavera (Low-Potassium)

   - **Dinner:** Roasted Chicken Thighs with Vegetables

   - **Snack:** Rice Cakes with Hummus

- Day 27

  - **Breakfast:** Spinach and Feta Omelette

  - **Lunch:** Quinoa Tabbouleh Salad

  - **Dinner:** Vegetable Curry (Low-Potassium)

  - **Snack:** Homemade Fruit Sorbet

- Day 28

  - **Breakfast:** Overnight Oats with Apples and Cinnamon

  - **Lunch:** Chicken Caesar Salad (Low-Potassium)

  - **Dinner:** Stuffed Bell Peppers (Variation)

  - **Snack:** Frozen Grapes or Berries

- Day 29

  - **Breakfast:** Fruit and Yogurt Parfait

  - **Lunch:** Tuna Salad Sandwich on Whole-Grain Bread

  - **Dinner:** Grilled Chicken with Roasted Vegetables

  - **Snack:** Greek Yogurt with Berries

- Day 30

  - **Breakfast:** Pancakes Made with Almond Flour

  - **Lunch:** Vegetable Wrap with Hummus

  - **Dinner:** Baked Salmon with Roasted Asparagus and Quinoa

- **Snack:** Cottage Cheese with Fruit

Additional Meal Plan Tips

- **Don't be afraid to switch things up:** Feel free to swap recipes or ingredients to keep your meals interesting and enjoyable.

- **Listen to your body:** Pay attention to your hunger cues and adjust your portion sizes accordingly.

- **Don't be afraid to ask for help:** If you're struggling to follow a low-potassium meal plan, don't hesitate to reach out to a registered dietitian or healthcare provider for guidance.

- **Celebrate your successes:** Acknowledge your progress and reward yourself for sticking to your low-potassium diet.

- **Enjoy the process:** Cooking and eating healthy meals can be a rewarding experience. Take your time and savor each bite.

CONCLUSION

As you embark on your journey to a healthier, happier you, **"The Complete Low Potassium Cookbook for Seniors"** is your trusted companion. With a wealth of delicious and easy-to-follow recipes, this cookbook empowers you to take control of your health and enjoy a vibrant life.

Remember, managing hyperkalemia doesn't mean sacrificing flavor or enjoyment. With a little creativity and planning, you can create meals that are both nutritious and delicious. So, don't let the fear of dietary restrictions hold you back. Embrace the opportunity to discover new flavors, explore different cuisines, and nourish your body in a way that supports your overall well-being.

The journey to better health starts here. With **"The Complete Low Potassium Cookbook for Seniors,"** you have the tools and knowledge to make every meal a delicious and fulfilling experience.

Acknowledgments

Thank you for choosing **"The Complete Low Potassium Cookbook for Seniors."** Your support means the world to me. Please take a moment to leave a review and share this cookbook with others who may benefit. Your feedback helps me continue to create delicious and informative recipes.

Made in the USA
Columbia, SC
16 December 2024

49664187R00070